Love Is Forever

Love Is Forever

Copyright © 1990
Brownlow Publishing Company, Inc.
6309 Airport Freeway
Ft. Worth, Texas 76117
ISBN 1-877719-07-2

A Special Gift

For _Ruth_

By _Gail_

August 7 19 _99_

Blessings From the Heart

Love Is Forever

Leroy Brownlow

Brownlow

Brownlow Publishing Company

Brownlow Gift Books

A Few Hallelujahs for Your Ho-Hums
A Psalm in My Heart
As a Man Thinketh
Better Than Medicine — A Merry Heart
Children Won't Wait
Flowers for Mother
Flowers for You
Flowers of Friendship
Flowers That Never Fade
For Mom With Love
Give Us This Day
Grandpa Was a Preacher
It's a One-derful Life
Jesus Wept
Just Between Friends
Leaves of Gold
Love Is Forever
Making the Most of Life
The Fruit of the Spirit
The Greatest Thing in the World
The Other Wise Man
Thoughts of Gold — Wisdom for Living
Today and Forever
Today Is Mine
University of Hard Knocks
Your Special Day

Contents

Born to Love

WE ALL NEED LOVE. With all our complexities, we are not easy creatures to satisfy. We cannot meet the conditions of a satisfied life by gorging ourselves, lying down on the grass, and staring at the clouds. We have deeper needs than the brute, and the deepest one is love.

Babies cannot live on milk alone. They are born with a nature that requires love. There are many confirmed cases in which babies who received nourishment and shelter wasted away for a lack of love. With the passing of time the once-baby-now-adult has a greater need to give love than to receive it, to feel love more than he needs to be felt by it.

But we often think too much in terms of receiving love instead of giving it. However, we are not babies and as adults we need to scatter our affections around. We grownups like attention, too. We enjoy being pampered. It is gratifying to receive. But there is much more fulfillment and higher ecstasy in having a heart so filled with love that it finds more joy in giving than in receiving.

• *Our need for love is born within us.* Without the ministries of love we would perish. The child is born with a greater need to receive love than to give it; yet as he develops, the need becomes urgent in both respects.

The need of love is as universal as man himself. Wherever we walk, on every shore and in every clime, the need of love walks by our side. Our hearts cry out for affection. This implanted longing is proof that we are akin to God, for "God is love."

As the child receives love it learns to give love. That beginning emotion normally grows and grows until it embraces many people, even self, and many things. As this lovely force multiplies, it contributes to the spark and vigor of the individual, preparing him for a life a little lower than the angels. It is so essential and marvelous that Friedrich Von Schiller, in an appreciative and inquisitive mood, asked:

What is life without the radiance of love?

• *Love is not fantasy.* It is not just a topic for poets and philosophers. It is not just an idealistic longing for those who roam the silvery heavens. It is a state of the heart for *now* and *here,* for the people on earth.

> *True love's the gift which God has given*
> *To man alone beneath the heaven:*
> *It is not fantasy's hot fire,*
>   *Whose wishes, soon as granted, fly;*
> *It liveth not in fierce desire,*
>   *With dead desire it doth not die;*
> *It is the secret sympathy,*
> *The silver link, the silken tie,*
> *Which heart to heart and mind to mind*
> *In body and in soul can bind.*
>
> — SIR WALTER SCOTT

Loving is as real as living. It is the power we need to traverse life's pathway and to hurdle the obstacles. It is the cushion that softens the hard knocks we receive; it is the consideration that pillows the gentle blows we give.

Love controls conduct. No mad dog has it. And when a world turns mad, it is devoid of it.

It is not trite, therefore, to say that love will solve our problems, no more stereotyped than to say that food sustains life. Without food we die;

11

and without love we die a death worse than physical. Let's keep our values in their true perspective, and not depreciate them because the need has always existed. Let's rather mark up their value and live, live as exalted creatures on the high summit of tender attachment which many have not yet attained.

• *Love is the heart-beat topic that has been the thrilling theme of the sweetest eloquence through the centuries.* The Apostle Paul's immortal analysis in I Corinthians 13. Elizabeth Barrett Browning's "How Do I Love Thee." And John Keat's love letters to Fanny Brawne. But the sweetest words on this tuneful topic have not been spoken by orators nor penned by poets. They have been uttered in broken, unrhythmic language, and lived in unlettered deeds by a million unschooled people whose hearts overflowed with it. They knew the art of love. They learned it in the schoolroom of their own heart.

Love doesn't have to be wrapped in a college diploma. Neither does it have to speak in poetic terms. Love is that sentimental, but not always that educated. It utters a heart language, and no one group has the exclusive possession of that kind of heart.

Seas have their source,
* and so have shallow springs;*
And love is love, in beggars as in kings.
— SIR EDWARD DYER

Love is available to all. That lets each speak love in his own way and live it in the bounds of his own practicality. That permits each to demonstrate it, and that is the prettiest poetry and the grandest elocution.

Love is simple. The centuries have passed. The profoundest philosophers have walked on platform and spoken. The most accomplished poets have taken pen and written. But no human being has ever put together a stronger statement on love than the simple expression, "I love you." This is heart language.

All hearts in love use their own tongues.
— WILLIAM SHAKESPEARE

• *The most satisfying joy in all the world is in having a person dearer to you than your own self,* a person with whom you feel free to pour out and share your every thought, your every grief and your every joy; for it is with that person you feel a deep unity of spirits. This is love. For:

> *Love alone is capable of uniting living beings in such a way as to complete and fulfill them, for it alone takes them and joins them by what is deepest in themselves.*
>
> — PIERRE TEILHARD DE CHARDIN

What inspiration, what strength, what buoyancy it gives to know that if all the rest of the world should turn against you, rend you and forsake you, there is one person who will never wrong you by an unjust thought or unkind word or unmerciful deed, one person who will cling to you in poverty and in persecution, in disaster and in death, one person who will sacrifice all things for you and for whom you will sacrifice all things, even life. This person's welfare is your greatest concern. And it is with this person you expect never to be separated except by death. This is companionate love.

As surely as the sun rises in the heavens, the human spirit reaches its greatest heights of ecstasy when it roams the rapturous realm of romantic love.

In the stirrings of pure, sweet affection for another person, we experience expansion of the soul. That something within it we call love is too big for the soul's former size, and consequently something has to give, and we grow into a larger and nobler self.

• *Maturity is one of the chief traits of love.* Learning to love is an act of maturity. When love matures, so does the person. In Paul's brilliant and splendorous description of love, he explains:

When I was a child, I spake as a child, I understood as a child, I thought as a child: but when I became a man, I put away childish things.

— I CORINTHIANS 13:11

As we become more grown in love we outgrow our immaturity. We say the individual is a big, big person, and he is; he is too big to whimper, complain, nettle, find fault, or forever feel mistreated. His maturity lets him reach out of self and identify with another, and thus bear and share with the other person. Maturity enables us to stand in the other fellow's shoes, as it were, and to walk in them

and limp because of the pebble which the intoler-
ant never notice. The mature feel with others while
the immature only ache with their own needs.

• *The richer the personality, the easier it is for
love to compound itself,* even increasing in delight
and satisfaction with every enlargement. This is
natural, for love, the embodiment of all that is
good and pure, lives on love.

Whatever love we have — and it does come in
degrees — feed it and it will grow, and as it expands
so will our personality.

But with some, love is more difficult. The reason is: their concept of love was distorted in childhood, and today they have a false image of love.
They may see it as something selfish and demanding, cruel and domineering, an inconsistent way of
life more concerned with itself than with the one
they love. Of course, they experienced only a distortion of professed love. As a result, these people
now in adulthood meet love with resentment. For
all have a tendency to pull away from unpleasant
experiences.

The people who are scared of love rebound
against it. This is why some rebel at love and start
hating anyone who loves them, though they may

not be fully conscious of it. Sometimes this happens even toward the minister of a church who loves and serves them. The Apostle Paul said of such confused people, "Though the more abundantly I love you the less I be loved" (II Corinthians 12:15). This, of course, is not the normal reaction.

The normal pattern is expressed in the same Bible, a super book on psychology, in a more reciprocal reaction: "We love him, because he first loved us" (I John 4:19). This is the normal response to love.

So when a person finds it hard to love, perhaps something went awry in his development. The true self was stepped on. The fuller life of love was checked. But this condition is not hopeless. Nothing is hopeless with us for the simple reason we are human, we have intelligence, will and a soul, which enable us to replace selfishness with big-heartedness, and hate with love.

• *For us to love others properly we must first love ourselves rightly.* Of course, the correct balance must be kept. In correcting an imbalance, it is unfortunate that love for self has been attacked when it is actually a virtue essential to self-preservation. It is only a perversion of loving self that is the culprit.

The Second Commandment of the Law is based on self-love:

Thou shalt love thy neighbor as thyself.
— MATTHEW 22:39

This is proof that self-love when linked with a love for others is not evil.

By all means, each should love himself enough not to run himself down. Have you observed that some people glory in their downgradings ? This over-depreciation of self is a form of egotism that surfaces in opposing itself. It is a vanity that pulls itself down in a twisted effort to push itself up.

This lowering of self, however, does not stop with self. The self-lowered person begins to have trouble with others. Cain had strife with his brother Abel because first of all he had strife with himself. Controlled self-love could have saved Cain from uncontrolled brother-hate.

It was actually self-hate that led Cain to destroy his brother, himself and the first home. Charles Swain said, "Home is where there's one to love us." So when hate replaced love, the walls stood but the home was gone. It left Cain homeless with no lot but to roam the earth as a fugitive and a vagabond.

A principal reason some people are so bitter toward humanity is they don't like themselves. It stands to reason that no one could love another when he does not even like himself.

Hence, we must first learn to love ourselves:
— By seeing ourselves as the object of
   God's love, a creature worth loving.
— By seeing love as it really is.
— By expecting of ourselves only that
   which is reasonable.
— By refusing to compare ourselves with
   more fortunate people.
— By accepting ourselves as we are.
— By keeping a clear conscience.
— By being the kind of persons we can
   be proud of.

All of this encourages self-respect and self-love, and then we will be ready to love others.

The Miracle of Love

The sense of the world is short,—
Long and various the report,—
To love and be beloved;
Men and gods have not outlearned it;
And, how oft soe'er they've turned it,
'Tis not to be improved.

—RALPH WALDO EMERSON

It is love that gives things their value.

—C. CARRETTO

One heart, one mind
    One soul, and one desire,
A kindred fancy,
    and a sister fire
Of thought and passion;
    these can love inspire:
This makes a heaven of earth;
    for this is Love.

—CHAMBER'S JOURNAL

Love is a miracle
Making hearts sing,
Love is a beautiful,
Wonderful thing.
Love is a precious gift
Worth more than gold,
And love that is true love
Never grows old.

—HELEN FARRIES

Love can hope where reason would despair.

—LYTTELTON

Wheresoever a man seeketh his own,
   there he falleth from love.

—THOMAS A KEMPIS

Love is the only force capable of
   transforming an enemy into a friend.

—M.L. KING

Let the burden never be so heavy,
   love makes it light.

—R. BURTON

22

"*How do I love thee?*"
   Let me count the ways.
I love thee to the depth
   and breadth and height
My soul can reach, when feeling out of sight
For the ends of Being, and ideal grace.
I love thee to the level of every day's
Most quick need, by sun and candle-light,
I love thee freely as men strive for Right;
I love thee purely as they turn from Praise.
I love thee with the passion put to use
In my old griefs, and with thy
   childhood's faith.

—ELIZABETH BARRETT BROWNING

The light of love shines over all,
Of love, that says not mine and thine,
But ours, for ours is thine and mine.

—HENRY WADSWORTH LONGFELLOW

They do not love that do not show their love.

—HEYWOOD

If there is anything better than to be loved
   it is loving.

—RALPH WALDO EMERSON

Love, like a lamp, needs to be fed out of the oil of another's heart, or its flame burns low.

—HENRY WARD BEECHER

The heart that loves is always young.

*Love rules without a sword,
Love binds without a cord.*

To love anyone is nothing else than to wish that person good.

—THOMAS AQUINAS

Love spends his all, and still hath store.

—P.J. BAILEY

Love thrives in the face of all life's hazards, save one—neglect.

—J.D. BRYDEN

Love is love's reward.

—JOHN DRYDEN

While faith makes all things possible,
it is love that makes all things easy.

—EVAN HOPKINS

Not where I breathe,
But where I love,
I live.

—R. SOUTHEY

Spring bursts today,
For love is risen
and all the earth's at play.

—CHRISTINA ROSSETTI

Thou art my life, my love, my heart,
The very eyes of me:
And hast command every part
To live and die for thee.

—R. HERRICK

Love is the only power that can overcome
the self-centeredness that is inherent
in being alive.

—ARNOLD TOYNBEE

25

For Love's Sake

*L*ove is the dynamic force that pulls together and solidifies the inner self, preventing our restless and resentful runs in many directions to do battle on many fronts.

In contrast, there is no disturber and disintegrator like hate. We can have no peace when we are torn apart, and there can be no internal unity except when it centers around love. Love is the magnetic center of human behavior; and, like the North Pole attracts the compass, man when threatened by the shattering urges of resentment and vindictiveness can be pulled together and integrated by love. Affection is the unifying power of personality which unites one into a whole person and prepares him to pursue a straight course of goodwill. And it is only in this oneness and on this course that we can find peace, tranquility and happiness.

Love makes the difference. I have never seen a person of love who wasn't happy. I have never seen a person of hate who wasn't miserable. The power of love is not to be questioned.

*Doubt, if you will, the being who loves you,
Woman or dog, but never doubt love itself.*
— ALFRED DE MUSSET

• *Love is the giver of good things, both to the giver
and the receiver.* If it is more blessed to give than to
receive (and it is), then the lover is set up to truly
receive; for he is the world's most liberal giver, and
consequently the world's most abundant receiver.

While on the other hand, hate which encourages negative reactions withholds from the hater
what he really wants.

A child may refuse to eat when he is hungry.
This negative reaction may cause him to reject
many other requests, even though he would like to
do them. It is a way of getting back at a world he
feels compelled to battle. The cause — resentment.

Another child would seal her lips and refuse to
say a word when spoken to in public with her par-
ents. She could not be coaxed to speak. Another
negative reaction which separated her from the
society of which she really craved to be a part.

This is an unfortunate lifestyle recoil carried
over into adulthood by many people. They hurt

themselves more than the whole world can harm them. In this twisted pattern they always feel left out; and they are, but they exclude themselves.

How unrealistic for people to maintain a feeling that denies them the very things they want.

Love changes this. When animosity is replaced with affection, it is easy for us to take our place in a more inviting society where we can find a world of good things.

• *Love, bringing new sight to old eyes, sees the best in every person.* It gives the benefit of the doubt. One of love's sweet virtues is its inclination to be blind to faults.

> *Love to faults is always blind,*
> *Always is to joy inclin'd,*
> *Lawless, wing'd, and unconfin'd,*
> *And breaks all chains from every mind.*
> —WILLIAM BLAKE

Maybe we should rather say that love which appears blind has the best vision of all. It sees beyond the error and views the extenuating circumstances.

Love does not vary when it recognizes imperfection.

Love is not love
Which alters when it alteration finds,
Or bends with the remover to remove:
O, no! is an ever-fixed mark
That looks on tempests and is never shaken.
—WILLIAM SHAKESPEARE

Instead of changing, love mercifully curtains the weakness.

For love covereth a multitude of sins.
—I PETER 4:8

This makes life so much sweeter, for the best of us are susceptible to faults.

Love is not harsh and censorious. He loves me best who judges me less. The question propounded by the Master Teacher is ever relevant: "And why beholdest thou the mote that is in thy brother's eye, but considerest not the beam that is in thine own eye?"

• *Love is active.* Love is kind, and kindness is goodness in motion. While it is true that sometimes love is silent, yet that silence is filled with stirrings.

When silence speaks for love
she has much to say.
—RICHARD GARNETT

When Peter betrayed Jesus, "the Lord turned, and looked upon Peter," without saying a word. The love of Christ was silent, but it was also active: the Lord looked. That look was the movement Peter needed. It helped him to come to himself. Love is always active in its helpfulness.

When the Good Samaritan saw the man who had been robbed, beaten and left half dead by the wayside, he had compassion upon him.

A pity beyond all telling
Is hid in a heart of love.
—WILLIAM BUTLER YEATS

But there was more than the going out of his heart, his hands also went out. He ministered to the victim's wounds, took him to an inn and cared for him that night, and then made arrangements for his continued care. This is love's behavior. It is active.

When the need arises, love spontaneously and unmeditatively moves to help.

31

A spring of love gushed from my heart
And I blessed them unaware.

—SAMUEL TAYLOR COLERIDGE

• *Love grants freedom.* It is not possessive. One of the most convincing manifestations of pure love is the freedom it grants another.

Demanding that your friend cut off all other friendships and shower all attention on you is not true love. Such a distortion of love is the reverting back to childhood.

One woman in speaking of another said, "I can't afford to become a close friend of hers. She wouldn't let me have other friends. I would have to be with her constantly. She gives no freedom." The woman who was passed by would be quick in asserting her love, but true love grants freedom. Love doesn't draw a circle that small.

I know a woman who refuses to do very much to help herself, because she gets a perverted satisfaction from watching her children bow and scrape in their attentions toward her. She says, "They should put me first. It is their duty. I'm their mom."

Poor woman! She has missed the point of service through love. She has bound a duty relationship upon them. Think how much more enjoyable life would be, if she would reverse the order as much as age and time permit, and serve rather than be served.

Another widow says, "I want my children to be free to live their own lives. I love them too much to be demanding. I have served them a long time, and if God wills I prefer to go on through life in the same manner." Here was love that granted freedom.

I am acquainted with a woman who nags and persecutes her husband when he goes fishing or golfing which is not often. She feels neglected. She harps on the idea that if he loved her, he would not do it. Her love of self permits no latitude for him.

Another wife gets joy out of her husband's recreational activities because it brings joy to him. She loves him more than self, too much to be selfish, too much to tie him to her apron strings.

Then there is the case of the man who resents his wife's various social activities during the day. He says that she ought to be at home. He would imprison her.

But I know another man who rejoices in his wife's outside activities. His love lends purpose and fulfillment to her life.

Love is no browbeating, domineering quality. It is no choking process. It does not smother all human dignity. It is rather a big soft kiss of consideration that frees one to naturally respond to the lover.

• *Love is the energy-maker.* Love is the power to release energy and keep going when the person of hate has already fatigued out. Of course, both love and hate are active forces in every person's life, but love should be the dominant power.

There is no way for love to exist without the existence of hate. Love is positive. Hate is negative. And every positive has a negative, and this is no less true of love. If we love goodness, we must of necessity hate evil. By the same measurement, if we love truth, we hate falsehood. The Bible aptly states it this way: "Thou lovest righteousness, and hatest wickedness" (Psalms 45:7). Yet, the Bible is unique in its advocacy of love as the compelling power in the heart. The world turns through a positive force while it negates that which conflicts with it.

34

• *The bravest fearlessness is born of love.* Our metal is largely mental. What affects the mind affects the courage. Every strong backbone grows out of the heart, and what influences it most is love.

A mother ran into a burning house and grabbed her helpless baby from the crib. As she reached the door, her hair was scorched, her dress was on fire, but the baby was saved. She exemplified a courage that knew no limits because she had a love that knew no bounds. Her metal was mental. Her heroics sprang from her love.

A father and a son were cleaning out an old water well. As sometimes happens, a deadly gas began to fill the well. They gasped for breath. They struggled. The father motioned for the men at the top to lower the large bucket. Both climbed in and they were being drawn up. But the rope cracked, too much strain for too much weight. A strand broke and another, then the father jumped and fell to the bottom. The son was lifted to safety. The father died to save the son. Unlimited courage due to unbounded love. Nothing unusual — just a law of love.

• *Love is the way of life for everyone toward everyone, even enemies.*

Love is an emotion regulated by the lover rather than the person being loved. Our love for someone is dependent upon who we are, not upon the merits of the recipient This is why God loves everyone — not that everyone is lovable. With this insight, we see that it is not unreasonable to love an enemy. And the more we do it, the more we change ourselves into the image of God.

Perhaps many people we associate with have traits we do not like — braggarts, manipulators, egotists, climbers, bullies, oppressors — but we can still love them for love's sake; and in so doing we will be blessed much more than they.

After all, none is perfect, not you, not me. Yet all of us need to be loved. But those who extend it will have to be people like you and me who have touched earth as well as heaven.

But friend to me
He is all fault who hath no fault at all.
For who loves me must have a touch of earth.
　　　　　　　　　　　　—ALFRED TENNYSON

Tokens of Love

You can give without loving,
but you can never love without giving.

The great acts of love are done by those
who are habitually performing small acts
of kindness.

We pardon to the extent that we love.

Love is knowing that even when
you are alone, you will never
be lonely again.

The great happiness of life is the conviction
that we are loved, loved for ourselves,
or rather loved in spite of ourselves.
— VICTOR HUGO

Love is the poetry of the senses.
— HONORÉ DE BALZAC

*The way to love anything
is to realize it might be lost.*
— G.K. CHESTERTON

Until I truly loved, I was alone.
— CAROLINE SHERIDAN NORDON

*One word frees us of all the weight
and pain of life: that word is love.*
— SOPHOCLES

*Love is that condition in which the
happiness of another person
is essential to your own joy.*
— ROBERT A. HEINLIN

*Love is the gentle smile
upon the lips of beauty.*
— KAHIL GIBRAN

*Love cures people —
both the ones who give it
and the ones who receive it.*
— KARL MENNINGER

Those who love deeply never grow old;
they may die of old age,
but they die young.
— ARTHUR WING PINERO

We do not fall in love; we grow in love,
and love grows in us.
— KARL MENNINGER

We are shaped and fashioned
by what we love.
— GOETHE

We are all born for love.
It is the principle of existence,
and its only end.
— BENJAMIN DISRAELI

Do not be afraid of showing your affection.
Be warm and tender,
thoughtful and affectionate.
Men are more helped by sympathy,
than by service; love is more than money,
and a kind word will give more pleasure
than a present.
— JOHN LUBBOCK

*In dreams and love
there are no impossibilities.*
— JANOS ARANY

There is no remedy for love but to love more.
— HENRY DAVID THOREAU

Love is the enchanted dawn of every heart.
— ALPHONSE DE LAMARTINE

*The pleasure of love is in loving,
and one is happier in the passion one feels
than in the passion one arouses in
another.*
— LA ROCHEFOUCAULD

*That best portion of a good man's life,
His little, nameless, unremembered acts
Of kindness and of love.*
— WILLIAM WORDSWORTH

How vast a memory has love.
— ALEXANDER POPE

*That love is all there is,
Is all we know of love.*
— EMILY DICKINSON

40

To love for the sake of being loved is human,
but to love for the sake of loving is angelic.
— ALPHONSE DE LAMARTINE

Freely we serve, because we freely love.
— JOHN MILTON

Man's love is of man's life a thing apart,
'Tis woman's whole existence.
— LORD BYRON

Let those love now
who never loved before;
Let those who always loved,
now love the more.
— THOMAS PARNELL

If you loved me ever so little,
I could bear the bonds that gall.
— ALGERNON CHARLES SWINBURNE

So dear I love him, that with him all deaths
I could endure, without him live no life.
— JOHN MILTON

41

And This Is Love

*T*HIS PASSION OF WHICH we speak, though it begins with the young, forsakes not the old, or rather suffers no one who is its servant to grow old, but makes the aged participators of it not less than the tender maiden, though in a different and nobler sort.

No man ever forgot the visitations of that power to his heart and brain, which created all things anew; which was the dawn in him of music, poetry and art; which made the face of nature radiant with purple light, the morning and the night varied enchantments; when a single tone of one voice could make the heart bound; when he became all eye when one was present, and all memory when one was gone; when the youth becomes a watcher of windows and studious of a glove, a veil, or a ribbon.

In the noon and the afternoon of life we still throb at the recollection of days when happiness was not happy enough, but must be drugged with the relish of pain and fear; for he touched the secret of the matter who said of love:

All other pleasures are not worth its pains.

And when the day was not long enough, but the night too must be consumed in keen recollections; when the head boiled all night on the pillow with the generous deed it resolved on; when the moonlight was a pleasing fever and the stars were letters and the flowers ciphers and the air was coined into song; when all business seemed an impertinence, and all the men and women running to and fro in the streets, mere pictures.

Love rebuilds the world for the youth. It makes all things alive and significant. Every bird on the boughs of the trees sings now to his heart and soul. The notes are almost articulate. The clouds have faces as he looks on them. The trees of the forest, the waving grass and the peeping flowers have grown intelligent; and he almost fears to trust them with the secret which they seem to invite. Yet nature soothes and sympathizes.

The like force has the passion over all his nature. It expands the sentiment; it makes the clown gentle and gives the coward heart. Into the most pitiful and abject it will infuse a heart and courage to defy the world. He is a new man, with new perceptions, new and keener purposes, and a religious solemnity of character and aims.

Little think the young and maiden who are glancing at each other across crowded rooms with eyes so full of mutual intelligence, of the precious fruit long hereafter to proceed from this new, quiet external stimulus. From exchanging glances, they advance to acts of courtesy, of gallantry, then to fiery passion, to plighting troth and marriage. Passion beholds its object as a perfect unit.

Life, with this pair, has no other aim, asks no more, than Juliet—than Romeo. The lovers delight in endearments, in avowals of love, in comparisons of their regards. When alone, they solace themselves with the remembered image of the other. Does that other see the same star, the same melting cloud, read the same book, feel the same emotion, that now delights me?

But the lot of humanity is on these children. Danger, sorrow and pain arrive to them as to all. Love prays. It makes covenants with Eternal Power in behalf of this dear mate. The union which is thus effected and which adds a new value to every atom in nature is yet a temporary state. Not always can flowers, pearls, poetry, protestations, nor even home in another heart, content the soul that dwells in clay. It arouses itself at last from these endearments, as toys, and puts on the harness and aspires to vast and universal aims. The soul which is in the soul of each, craving a perfect beatitude, detects incongruities in the behavior of the other. Hence arise surprise, expostulation and pain.

Yet that which drew them to each other was signs of loveliness, signs of virtue; and these virtues are there, however eclipsed. They appear and reappear and continue to attract. This repairs the wounded affection. As life wears on, it proves a game of permutation of the parties to employ all the resources of each and acquaint each with the strength and weakness of the other. For it is the nature and end of this relation that they should represent the human race to each other..

The world rolls; the circumstances vary every hour. Their once flaming regard is sobered by time in either breast, it becomes a thorough good understanding. They resign each other without complaint to the good offices which man and woman are severally appointed to discharge in time. At last they discover that all which at first drew them together—those once sacred features, that magical play of charms—was deciduous, had a prospective end, like the scaffolding by which the house was built; and the purification of the intellect and the heart from year to year is the real marriage. And this is love.

—RALPH WALDO EMERSON

(abridged)

annah,

Hello! How are you?
doing quite well. I want
thank you for the beautiful
birthday present. I love it!

Thank you

M...

Endearments –
Letters from the Heart

Robert Browning to Elizabeth Barrett Browning
After Their Marriage

You will only expect a few words—what will those be? When the heart is full it may run over, but the real fullness stays within.

You asked me yesterday "if I should repent?" Yes —my own Ba, —I could wish all the past were to do over again, that in it I might somewhat more, — never so little more, conform in the outward homage, to the inward feeling. What I have professed . . . (for I have performed nothing) seems to fall short of what my first love required even—and when I think of this moment's love . . . I could repent, as I say. Words can never tell you, however, —form them, transform them any way, how perfectly dear you are to me—perfectly dear to my heart and soul.

I look back, and in every one point, every word and every gesture, every letter, every silence—you have been entirely perfect to me—I would not change one word, one look.

My hope and aim are to preserve this love, not to fall from it—for which I trust to God who procured it for me, and doubtless can preserve it.

Enough now, my dearest, own Ba! You have given me the highest, completest proof of love that ever one human being gave another. I am all gratitude— and all pride (under the proper feeling which ascribes pride to the right source) all pride that my life has been so crowned by you.

God bless you—prays—your very own R.

Ludwig Van Beethoven
to His "Immortal Beloved"

Good morning

Though still in bed my thoughts go out to you, my Immortal Beloved, now and then joyful- ly, then sadly, waiting to learn whether or not fate will hear us.

I can live only wholly with you or not at all —yes, I am resolved to wander so long away from you until I can fly to your arms and say that I am really at home, send my soul enwrapped in you into the land of spirits. —Yes, unhappily it must be so—you will be the more resolved since you know my fidelity—to you, no one can ever again possess my heart—none—never.

Oh, God! why is it necessary to part from one whom one so loves and yet my life in W. (Vienna) is now a wretched life—your love makes me at once the happiest and the unhappiest of men—at my age, I need a steady, quiet life—can that be under our conditions?

My angel, I have just been told that the mail coach goes every day—and I must close at once so that you may receive the letter at once.

Be calm, only by a calm consideration of our existence can we achieve our purpose to live together—be calm—love me—today—yesterday—what tearful longings for you—you—you—my life—my all—farewell—Oh continue to love me—never misjudge the most faithful heart of

> your beloved Lover
> ever thine
> ever mine
> ever for each other.

John Keats to Fanny Brawne

I never knew before, what such love as you have made me feel, was; I did not believe in it; my Fanny was afraid of it, lest it should burn me up. But if you will fully love me, though there may be some fire 'twill not be more than we can bear when moistened and bedewed with Pleasures . . .

I love you the more in that I believe you have liked me for my own sake and for nothing else. I have met with women whom I really think would like to be married to a Poem and to be given away by a Novel. Ever yours, my love!

Another Letter from Keats to Fanny Brawne

I have no limits now to my love. I have been astonished that men could die martyrs of religion. I have shuddered at it. I shudder no more. I could be martyred for my religion—love is my religion—I could die for you. My creed is love and you are its only tenet. You have ravish'd me away by a power I cannot resist . . . . My love is selfish. I cannot breathe without you . . . . Yours for ever.

Love at Home

House Blessing

Bless the four corners of this house,
　　And be the lintel blest;
And bless the hearth,
　　　and bless the board,
　　And bless each place of rest;
And bless the door that opens wide
　　To stranger, as to kin;
And bless each crystal windowpane
　　That lets the starlight in;
And bless the rooftree overhead,
　　And every sturdy wall.
The peace of man, the peace of God,
　　The peace of love on all.
　　　　　　　—ARTHUR GUITERMAN

Thus let me hold thee to my heart,
　　and every care resign:
And we shall never, never part,
　　my life—my all that's mine!
　　　　　　　—OLIVER GOLDSMITH

Better to have the love of one
Than smiles like morning dew;
Better to have a living seed
Than flowers of every hue.

—LEIGH HUNT

A house is built of logs and stone,
    Of tiles and posts and piers;
A home is built of loving deeds
    That stand a thousand years.

—VICTOR HUGO

To make a man happy, treat him like a
    dog—plenty of affection and a loose
    leash.

—C. CHARISSE

Seeing eye to eye in marriage often
    requires the bigger person
    to bend a bit.

—COLLIE

Better is a dinner of herbs where love is
    than a stalled ox and hatred therewith.

—PROVERBS 15:17

Marriage is not a thing of nature but a gift of God.

—MARTIN LUTHER

Husbands who have the courage to be tender, enjoy marriages that mellow through the years.

—B. FRANCIS

Marriage is our last, best chance to grow up.

—J. BARTH

Success in marriage is more than finding the right person: it is a matter of being the right person.

—BRICKNER

A happy marriage is a union of two good forgivers.

Kissing is a means of getting two people so close together that they can't see anything wrong with each other.

—G. YASENAK

*Husband and wife come to look
alike at last.*

—OLIVER WENDALL HOLMES

*It takes years to marry completely two
hearts, even of the most loving. A
happy wedlock is a long falling in love.*

—T. PARKER

*A successful marriage requires falling in
love many times—with the same
person.*

*If two people who love each other let a
single instant wedge itself between
them, it grows—it becomes a month,
a year, a century; it becomes too late.*

—JEAN GIRAUDOUX

*Marrying for love may be a bit risky, but
it is so honest that God can't help but
smile on it.*

—JOSH BILLINGS

*Something else every couple should save
for their old age is their marriage.*

—IMOGENE FEY

The light that shines the farthest shines
the brightest near home.

Two souls with but a single thought.
two hearts that beat as one.
—FRIEDRICH HALM

No man knows what the wife of his
bosom is—what a ministering angel
she is, until he has gone with her
through the fiery trials of this world.
—WASHINGTON IRVING

Love at Home

There is beauty all around
When there's love at home;
There is joy in every sound
When there's love at home.
Peace and plenty here abide,
Smiling sweet on every side;
Time doth softly, sweetly glide
When there's love at home.

God, the best maker of all marriages,
Combine your hearts in one.
—WILLIAM SHAKESPEARE

57

Love's Prayer

Lord,

Make me an instrument of Thy peace
Where there is hatred let me sow love;
Where there is injury, pardon;
Where there is doubt, faith;
Where there is despair, hope;
Where there is darkness, light; and
Where there is sadness, joy.

LOVE'S PRAYER

O Divine Master,

Grant that I may not so much
Seek to be consoled as to console;
To be understood as to understand;
To be loved as to love;
For it is in giving that we receive;
It is in pardoning that we are
pardoned; and
It is in dying that we are born to
eternal life.

— ST. FRANCIS OF ASSISI

The Greatest Thing in the World

He who is filled with love is filled with God himself.

——St. Augustine

The God of love my shepherd is,
And he that doth me feed:
While he is mine and I am his
What can I want or need.

——G. Herbert

Human love would never have the power
it has were it not rooted in an express
image of God.

——J. Mouroux

Thou shalt love the Lord thy God with all thy heart, and with all thy soul, and with all thy mind. This is the first and great commandment. And the second is like unto it, thou shalt love thy neighbor as thyself.

—Matthew 22:37-39

The true measure of loving God is to love him without measure.

—Bernard of Clairvaux

Any old woman can love God better than a doctor of theology can.

—St. Bonaventure

Divine love is a sacred flower, which in its early bud is happiness, and in its full bloom is heaven.

—Eleanor Louisa Hervey

He that loveth not, knoweth not God; for God is love.

—I John 4:8

*The love of wealth makes bitter men; the
love of God, better men.*

—W.L. HUDSON

*The rock of divine human love is deeper
down than the human buildings that
have been reared upon it.*

—ALEXANDER MACLAREN

*But as touching brotherly love ye need
not that I write unto you: for ye
yourselves are taught of God to love
one another.*

—I THESSALONIANS 4:9

*Human things must be known to be
loved: but Divine things must be loved
to be known.*

—BLAISE PASCAL

*A new commandment I give unto you,
That you love one another; as I have
loved you, that you also love one
another. By this shall all men know
that ye are my disciples, if ye have
love one to another.*

—JOHN 13:34,35

To love as Christ loves is to let our love be a practical and not a sentimental thing.

—CHARLES VILLIERS STANFORD

I know not where his islands lift
Their fronded palms in air;
I only know I cannot drift
Beyond His love and care.

—JOHN GREENLEAF WHITTIER

See that ye love one another with a pure heart fervently.

—I PETER 1:22

Before we can minister in love, we must be mastered by love.

For God so loved the world, that he gave his only begotten Son, that whosoever believeth in him should not perish, but have everlasting life.

—JOHN 3:16

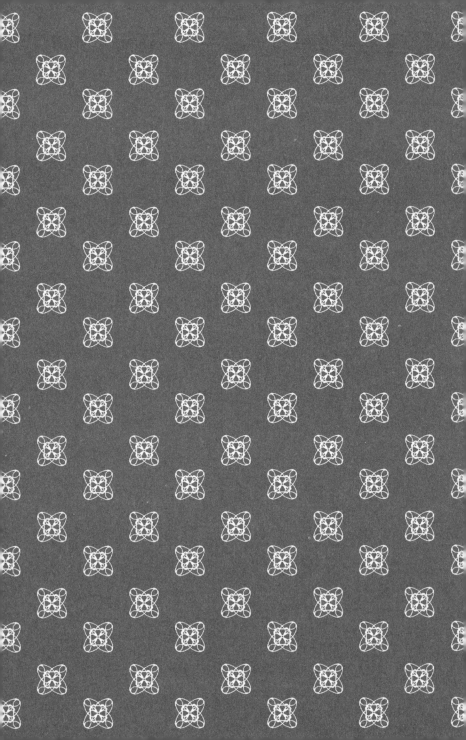